Buses, Coaches & Recollections

Contents

Introduction	3
Scotland	4
England	9
Wales	41
Guernsey	46
1969 No 1 Records	16
1969 Happenings	32, 35, 44, 47, 48
1969 Arrivals & Departures	47
Index of locations and operators	48

© Henry Conn 2015

All rights reserved. No part of this publication may be reproduced, stored in a retrieval system or transmitted, in any form or by any means, electronic, mechanical, photocopying, recording or otherwise, without prior permission in writing from Silver Link Publishing Ltd.

First published in 2015

British Library Cataloguing in Publication Data

A catalogue record for this book is available from the British Library.

Acknowledgments

A large number of the illustrations in this book are from the camera of Bob Gell, without which, and the detailed notes on each slide, this book would not have been possible. My most sincere thanks to Bob.

The PSV Circle Fleet Histories for the operators in this book and a number of issues of *Buses Illustrated* were also vital sources of information.

ISBN 978 1 85794 457 0

Silver Link Publishing Ltd
The Trundle
Ringstead Road
Great Addington
Kettering
Northants NN14 4BW

Tel/Fax: 01536 330588
email: sales@nostalgiacollection.com
Website: www.nostalgiacollection.com

Printed and bound in the Czech Republic

About the author

My first recollections of public transport were early in 1958 in my home town of Aberdeen, travelling from our home in Mastrick to Union Street, then onwards by tram to Bridge of Dee. My interest in buses, trolleybuses and trams expanded to taking fleet numbers or registration numbers, and by the mid-1960s I had acquired a camera and began my collection. This interest continued through my family's moves from Aberdeen to Perth, Whitburn in West Lothian, Banbury, Swindon and Oxford by 1974.

My first job was with Customs & Excise, beginning in London with transfers to Oxford, Dover and Brighton. It was after I left Brighton that my enthusiasm for bus photography waned, and it never really returned apart from sporadic photography when I returned to Scotland in 1980. By this time I had left Customs & Excise and had returned to college in Cupar to study Agriculture. I met my future wife at this college and moved with her parents to Galloway, where I have lived very happily since 1983. To further my career I attended Aberdeen University to take a BSc Degree in Agriculture, and I successfully graduated in 1996. This led to me returning to the Civil Service with the Scottish Executive Rural Affairs Department, then through many changes to where I am now, working with Natural England as adviser to farmers on Environmental Schemes (three days a week from last July).

By 2010 I had a significant collection of transport views from the mid-1960s to the early 1980s. I met with Silver Link Publishing's editor Will Adams in Preston in early 2010 and was very kindly given the opportunity to write a volume on Buses, Trams and Trolleybuses in the Midlands. Since then I have continued to enjoy writing volumes on transport for Silver Link, this volume being my second in the 'Recollections' series looking at buses, trolleybuses and trams as well as significant events in a specific year.

Introduction

To many, including myself, 1969 was a good year, but not, however, for people in Northern Ireland or Vietnam. In Ulster it was the time when the 'Troubles' came again – the jailing of Unionist hardliner Rev Ian Paisley, the Battle of Bogside, the conviction for incitement to riot of Bernadette Devlin McAliskey MP, and finally the arrival and deployment of the British Army. Meanwhile in South East Asia the newly inaugurated Richard Nixon began the policy of 'Vietnamisation' that would, he told us, soon bring the troops home. It didn't. Instead, the anti-war campaign grew stronger, fuelled not a little by Seymour Hersh's revelation that US troops massacred 109 villagers in a place called My Lai. The name still resonates 40 years on, as does that of Sharon Tate, pregnant wife of Roman Polanski, murdered in August by Charles Manson.

For some, it was a year of coming to power: Yasser Arafat, elected leader of the Palestine Liberation Front, Golda Meir, Prime Minister of Israel, and in Libya, after the summary removal of King Idris, Colonel Gaddafi. Enter, too, Rupert Murdoch as the new owner of the News of the World, together with the Victoria Line, Concorde, Boeing's 747, the quartz watch, maxi skirts and, in San Francisco, the first Gap store.

Shopping was not quite the obsession it was to become; nor, too, were house prices, the average being £4,640. But wages, and the lengths unions would go to improve them, were becoming an issue – a teacher, for instance, earned about £1,650.

Sport, as ever, was a diversion and comfort. England were still world champions at football, Birmingham-born Ann Jones won Wimbledon, Scotland's Jackie Stewart was top Grand Prix driver, and Tony Jacklin, a 25-year-old lorry driver's son from Scunthorpe, was the first Briton to win golf's Open Championship in 18 years.

Pirate radio had gone, T-shirts from 1967's 'Summer of Love' had long since shrunk in the wash, the Beatles' gave their last performance on the Apple HQ roof, and they released their swansong LP, Abbey Road. The group whose first No 1 hit had introduced me to music had run out of good tunes, and out of patience with each other. Before the year ended, Paul McCartney would marry Linda Eastman, and John Lennon and Yoko Ono would stage their bed-in at a Montreal hotel and record the dirge called Give Peace A Chance. Woodstock, that August, seemed like the end of something.

Charles de Gaulle stood down from the presidency of France, and Dwight D. Eisenhower, architect of D-Day and the man who presided over America's years of innocent plenty, died. So too did Warner Brothers' Looney Tunes cartoon series – 'That's All Folks!'. The Krays were finally sent down at the Old Bailey, Sir Matt Busby left the manager's seat at Manchester United, and Brian Jones of the Rolling Stones was found dead in his swimming pool, something of a mystery to this day.

So why was 1969 a good year for me? I left the village in West Lothian that I detested and moved to Banbury, and the time I spent there was full of laughter and happiness.

Enjoy the nostalgia!

Title page: **DUMFRIES** Crossing New Bridge in Dumfries on a local service to Lochside on 13 September 1969 is No 1712 (TCS 160), an ECW-bodied Bristol FLF6G new in 1962. The car behind is a brand new H-registered Morris Minor saloon. *Author's collection*

The last convertible/tourer Minor left the production line on 18 August 1969 and the saloon models were discontinued the following year.

The first ever episode of Scooby-Doo, Where Are You? was broadcast on this day on CBS.

Photo	DESTINATIONS
1	DUMFRIES (Title page)
2	DUNDEE
3	DUNDEE
4	DUNDEE
5	PAISLEY
6	PAISLEY
7	DALBEATTIE
8	CUMNOCK
9	SANQUHAR
10	LEEDS
11	LEEDS
12	LEEDS
13	BRADFORD
14	BRADFORD
15	BRADFORD
16	HALIFAX
17	HALIFAX
18	HALIFAX
19	HALIFAX
20	HALIFAX

Scotland

DUNDEE Between March and April 1953 ten Weymann-bodied Daimler CVD6s entered service with Dundee Corporation. They were Nos 70 to 79 (CTS 629 to 638), and were Dundee's first 8-foot-wide buses, with Daimler 8.4-litre engines. Four survived until 1975 and were the last Daimler exposed-radiator buses in Scotland. This is No 70 (CTS 629) on learner duties on 20 September 1969; it was one of those that survived into 1975, when it was sold to Codona, a dealer in Ballieston. *Author's collection*

On this day, according to Allan Klein, John Lennon chose to tell the group that he was leaving the Beatles.

Buses, Coaches & Recollections 1969

Below: **DUNDEE** Standing at Shore Terrace in Docks Street on 3 July 1969 is No 72 (CTS 631), another of the Weymann-bodied CVD6s; it was sold for scrap in March 1973. In the background is No 145 (AYJ 375), a Barnard-bodied AEC Regent III that entered service in March 1950 and was sold for scrap in early 1971. *Author's collection*

On this day, Brian Jones, musician and a founder member of the Rolling Stones, drowned in a swimming pool at his home in Sussex.

Above: **DUNDEE** Nos 25 to 34 (CTS 125D to 134D) were built by Alexander in 1964 and delivered to Dundee during 1965; however, they were soon returned to Alexander where all ten were stored until 1966, when they were registered and put into service. This view of No 27 was taken on 8 July 1969. *Author's collection*

This day saw the first withdrawal of US troops from Vietnam.

PAISLEY This is Western SMT No 1148 (GCS 234) in Dunn Square, Paisley, on 31 May 1969, a Northern Counties-bodied Leyland PD2/20 new in June 1955. In February 1970 it was acquired by Alexander (Northern) and given the fleet number NRB 172; in September 1973 it was acquired for spares by Highland Omnibuses and sold for scrap soon afterwards. *Author's collection*

On this day John Lennon and Yoko Ono recorded **Give Peace a Chance** *and Stevie Wonder released* **My Cherie Amour.**

PAISLEY In 1965 McGill's of Barrhead took delivery of three Alexander-bodied Daimler CRG6LXs, CHS 721C to 723C; this is CHS 723C at Paisley Cross on 20 August 1969. The Western SMT bus in the background on service to Kilmacolm is No 1437 (LCS 972), an NCME-bodied Leyland PD3/3 new in 1958. *Author's collection*

A few months after this view was taken, on 13 November, Gerard Butler was born in Paisley.

Buses, Coaches & Recollections 1969

DALBEATTIE The last ECW-bodied Bristol LD6Gs were delivered to Western SMT in 1961, numbered 1628 to 1647 (RAG 394 to 413). This is No 1642 leaving Dalbeattie for Kippford on 8 August 1969. On the left, in the distance, is Criagnair Quarry, which was opened by the Trustees of Liverpool Dock to build their harbour. The quarry's granite was of a high standard and was in demand both for buildings and monuments. It was also used for kerbstones, setts and cobblestones throughout the UK. *Author's collection*

At 11.30am on this day Iain Macmillan famously photographed the Beatles on a zebra crossing in Abbey Road, London. The album Abbey Road was released on 26 September.

CUMNOCK Western SMT No 1873 (VCS 427) was an Alexander-bodied Albion LR1 new in 1963; at the date of this view, 14 August 1969, is was allocated to Cumnock depot and was on a journey picking up students going to the Barony College, Dumfries. *Author's collection*

On this day British troops are deployed in Northern Ireland following the disturbances at Bogside.

SANQUHAR is a small market town in the Nith Valley located almost directly halfway between Ayr and Dumfries on the A76. The small bus company of Leith of Sanquhar purchased a variety of second-hand single- and double-deckers from a number of operators. This is DRN 280, an all-Leyland PD2/3 new to Ribble in December 1950. Withdrawn in 1964, it was purchased by Cowley of Salford in April 1964, and acquired by Leith the following month; this view is dated 6 January 1969. I think the livery and bus look very smart – it was last licensed by Leith in June 1971. *Author's collection*

On 6 January 1969 the 'Waverley' railway route between Edinburgh and Carlisle via Galashiels and Hawick was closed to passenger traffic, as was the branch line from Leuchars to St Andrews.

Buses, Coaches & Recollections 1969

Photo	DESTINATIONS
10	HULL
11	HULL
12	HULL
13	HULL
14	HULL
15	HULL
16	BRADFORD
17	BRADFORD
18	BRADFORD
19	WAKEFIELD

England

HULL St Helen's Corporation was the only operator to purchase new Park Royal-bodied AEC Regent RTs to almost full London specification; 15 were delivered in 1950, and a further 25 in 1952. They gave years of service and some went to other operators after withdrawal, including Kingston-upon-Hull Corporation, which purchased a total of 19, nine in April 1962 and ten in October. On the right is Hull's No 144 (BDJ 66), new in 1950 and acquired by Hull in October 1962. It entered service in April 1963 and remained in the Corporation fleet until early 1971, when it was sold for scrap; it is seen here on a wet 10 May 1969. The overtaking bus is No 408 (FRH 408D), a Roe-bodied Leyland PDR1/1 Mark II new in February 1966, and sold for scrap in September 1982. *Bob Gell*

On this day Apollo 10 transmitted the first colour picture of Earth from space.

HULL During 1953 Hull took delivery of six Weymann 'Aurora'-bodied AEC Regent IIIs, Nos 336 to 341 (OKH 336 to 341), and good-looking buses they were too! This is No 341 at Hull Paragon railway station on 10 May 1969. Unfortunately, just after this view was taken No 341 was involved in an accident and never returned to service. *Bob Gell*

The Battle of Dong Ap Bia, also known as Hamburger Hill, began on this day during the Vietnam War. Although the heavily fortified Hill 937 was of little strategic value, US Command ordered its capture by a frontal assault, only to abandon it soon thereafter. The action caused both military and public outrage in America.

Buses, Coaches & Recollections 1969

Below: **HULL** Between February and December 1967 Hull purchased 36 Park Royal-bodied AEC Regent IIIs from Nottingham City Transport. This was exactly half of the batch of the 72 delivered new to Nottingham between June 1953 and October 1954. They were numbered 150 to 185, and had their front destination display altered to Hull specification and their rear destination panelled over before entering service. This is No 177 (OTV 142) on service 13 on the same wet May day; it was purchased in December 1967, entered service in June 1968, and sold for scrap in May 1973. *Bob Gell*

Above: **HULL** East Yorkshire No 632 (SRH 632) was one of a pair of Roe-bodied Leyland PD2/12s delivered in July 1955, and it is seen here behind the bus station on 10 May 1969. Both were withdrawn in November 1971, but while sister vehicle No 633 entered the service fleet, 632 was sold to North's at Sherburn-in-Elmet for scrap. *Bob Gell*

Five days after this photograph was taken a teenager known as Robert R. died in St Louis, Missouri, of a baffling medical condition. In 1984 it was identified as the first case of HIV/AIDS in North America.

HULL Also behind the bus station on that day was No 631 (SRH 631), a Roe-bodied Leyland PD2/12 with a 'Beverley Bar' roof new in 1955. This shape of roof was introduced in 1935, designed to pass under a Gothic arch at Beverley until 1970. Alongside on the left is No 726 (9726 AT), a Park Royal-bodied AEC Bridgemaster new in June 1962, which was sold to Farrar of Pocklington for scrap in July 1975. No 631 had suffered the same fate in September 1971. *Bob Gell*

In 1969 the Humber had its very own hovercraft service between Grimsby and Hull, named 'Hoverlink'. The service was provided by just one craft, christened Mercury, which ran from the Royal Dock Tidal Basin opposite the old herring quay at Grimsby to Hull. On a chilly February day in 1969, with only five paying passengers, the shiny new hovercraft left the Tidal Basin at 8.40am, 10 minutes late, but within half an hour, with speeds of up to an impressive 30 knots, it arrived safely in Hull. However, the river, with its unpredictable currents, was not entirely suitable for the modern lightweight hovercraft, and problems arose while docking the fragile craft in the confines of the Tidal Basin, with its stone quayside. On several occasions it was severely damaged and, being the only craft in service, was regularly taken out of service for lengthy and expensive repairs, leaving the three old coal-burning paddle steamers as the only reliable alternative option. This weakness contributed to the early demise of the short-lived Grimsby-Hull hovercraft service.

Below: **BRADFORD** This is West Riding No 1029 (BHL 380C), the last Guy Wulfrunian, showing the cream steering wheel fitted to the Roe H43/32F-bodied Wulfrunians when new. This view was taken in Bradford on 23 May 1969. *Author's collection*

On this day The Who released the concept album Tommy.

Above: **HULL** Also photographed on 10 May 1969, this is Connor & Graham's Park Royal-bodied Leyland PD2/12 (OCD 776), new in 1955 and acquired from Southdown in October 1968; it was repainted from the latter's apple green and cream livery into something akin to Brighton Hove & District red and cream. The bus remained with Connor & Graham until October 1972. C&G's Easington route was the only stage service into Hull run by an independent operator; it did not have access to the joint KHCT/EYMS bus station, but terminated some distance away in Baker Street, adjacent to Hull Central Library. *Bob Gell*

A few hours after this view was taken the Monty Python comedy group first got together.

BRADFORD As mentioned on page 7 of the 1968 volume in this series, Roe-bodied Daimler CVG6LX30 fleet Nos 572 to 576 were the first front-entrance double-deckers for the Leeds Corporation fleet, and were purchased in 1962 specifically for the Leeds to Bradford service, jointly operated with Bradford Corporation, on which Bradford mainly used front-entrance vehicles. Under the trolleybus wires in Bradford on 21 October 1969 is No 576 (576 CNW). *Author's collection*

Buses, Coaches & Recollections 1969

15

Below: **WAKEFIELD** This is Yorkshire Traction No 748 (RHE 448G), a 1969 Willowbrook-bodied Leyland Atlantean PDR1A/1, working the long Leeds-Wakefield-Barnsley-Sheffield service 67. The bus, one of four diverted from Devon General and still in that company's livery, is seen in Wakefield bus station on 4 August 1969. *Bob Gell*

A gallon of petrol cost 6s 2d, and the space probe Mariner 7 flew past Mars.

Above: **BRADFORD** Yorkshire Woollen purchased one batch of Albion Lowlander LR7s with Weymann bodywork in 1964, which would be that company's last new front-engined vehicles – I think the style of bodywork looks strangely uncomfortable on the chassis. This view of KHD 408 was taken on the same day as the previous view. *Author's collection*

On this day Willy Brandt became Chancellor of West Germany.

1969
No 1 Records

January
    Marmalade — Ob-la-di, Ob-la-da
    Fleetwood Mac — Albatross

February
    Move — Blackberry Way
    Amen Corner — (If Paradise Is) Half As Nice
    Peter Sarsted — Where Do You Go To My Lovely

March
    Marvin Gaye — I Heard It Through The Grapevine

April
    Desmond Dekker and the Aces — Israelites
    Beatles with Billy Preston — Get Back

June
    Tommy Roe — Dizzy
    Beatles — Ballad of John and Yoko

July
    Thunderclap Newman — Something In The Air
    Rolling Stones — Honky Tonk Women

August
    Zager and Evans — In The Year 2525

September
    Creedence Clearwater Revival — Bad Moon Rising

October
    Jane Birkin and Serge Gainsbourg — Je T'aime … Moi Non Plus
    Bobby Gentry — I'll Never Fall In Love Again
    Archies — Sugar Sugar

December
    Rolf Harris — Two Little Boys

WAKEFIELD On the right, standing in the bus station ready for a journey to Leeds on 2 July 1969, is West Riding No 895 (THL 895), a Roe-bodied Guy Wulfrunian new in June 1961; it would become one of the longer-lasting Wulfrunians, being withdrawn and sold in April 1972. Standing alongside is No 247 (RWY 516F), one of a batch of six NCME-bodied Daimler CRG6LXs new to Mexborough & Swinton in November 1967. That operator was absorbed by Yorkshire Traction on 1 October 1969 and No 247 was purchased by West Riding at around that time. The all-Leyland PD2/1 in the left background is No 700 (CHL 798), which was withdrawn and sold for scrap a month after this view was taken. *Author's collection*

In this year the Boeing 747 Jumbo jet made its first passenger flight carrying 191 people, most of them reporters and photographers, from Seattle to New York City.

Buses, Coaches & Recollections 1969

Photo	DESTINATIONS
20	DEWSBURY
21	DEWSBURY
22	BARNESLEY
23	HUDDERSFIELD
24	TODMORDEN
25	SHEFFIELD
26	SHEFFIELD
27	SHEFFIELD

Left: **DEWSBURY** In the bus station on the same day was Yorkshire Woollen No 54 (originally numbered 773), which when new in 1954 was a Metro-Cammell Weymann-bodied Leyland Motors Demonstrator built to Edinburgh Corporation specification, including the indicator layout; note also the lack of ventilators on the top deck. This bus was acquired by Yorkshire Woollen in 1956 and became very popular with the crews; it was noted as being very reliable. No 54 was withdrawn from service in late 1970 and sold for scrap in January 1971. *Bob Gell*

Right: **DEWSBURY** West Yorkshire took delivery of DWU 133 to DWU 137 and DWU 994 to DWU 999, ECW-bodied Bristol K5Gs, in 1939. During 1955 they were rebuilt with new chassis sides, incorporating overhauled running units and new 26-foot ECW bodies. Yorkshire Woollen hired six of these rebuilds in May 1969, and they ran with West Yorkshire fleet names. In August 1969 Yorkshire Woollen purchased all six, and seen in Dewsbury bus station on 4 August 1969 is OWT 201; when purchased this bus was given fleet number 152 and remained in service until September 1970, when it was sold for scrap. *Bob Gell*

The No 1 single for five weeks in July-August 1969 was **Honky Tonk Women** *by the Rolling Stones with* **Give Peace a Chance** *by The Plastic Ono Band at No 2.*

The Godfather *by Mario Puzo was first published in early August 1969.*

BARNSLEY County Motors of Lepton took delivery of four Roe-bodied Guy Arab IIIs in 1958, numbered 91 to 94 (NCX 176 to 179). On 1 October 1968 County Motors was acquired by Yorkshire Traction, and seen at Barnsley bus station on 4 August 1969 is NCX 178, in Yorkshire Traction livery with the fleet number 687. *Bob Gell*

HUDDERSFIELD County Motors served the area to the east of Huddersfield bounded by Dewsbury, Wakefield and Barnsley, operating from a depot at Waterloo in Huddersfield. The fleet had a pleasing livery of off-white and blue. This view of AVH 636B, a Roe-bodied Leyland PD3A/1 new in 1964, shows it still in County livery in the early spring of 1969, although the fleet had passed Yorkshire Traction the previous October. The Yorkshire Traction bus in the background is 3283 HE, also a Leyland PD3A, this time with Northern Counties bodywork. *Author's collection*

Below: **TODMORDEN** This is Todmorden No 18 (HWY 36), an all-Leyland PD2/1 new in 1950, still looking very smart in this view taken on 18 October 1969. *Author's collection*

On this day Rod Stewart joined the Small Faces.

Buses, Coaches & Recollections 1969

19

Right: **SHEFFIELD**
The Leyland Leopard was introduced in 1959, and the original 30-foot bus version was coded L1. During July 1960 Sheffield took delivery of five Weymann-bodied Leyland L1s, Nos 6 to 10 (6306 to 6310 W), and representing this batch on 15 November 1969 is No 8 (6308 W). *Author's collection*

On this day regular colour television broadcasts begin on BBC1 and ITV in the UK.

Above: **SHEFFIELD** Sheffield Joint Omnibus Committee's route 22 was from Sheffield to Holmesfield via Bradway, and was one of the very early conversions to one-person operation. This bus is No 1114 (TWE 114F), one of a batch of 16 Park Royal-bodied Leyland PDR1/1s new to Sheffield JOC in September 1968, and is was photographed in Sheffield bus station on 2 May 1969. *Author's collection*

The Queen Elizabeth 2's maiden voyage, from Southampton to New York, commenced on 2 May 1969, taking 4 days, 16 hours and 35 minutes. At the time of her retirement on 11 November 2008, the QE2 had sailed nearly 6 million miles, carried 2.5 million passengers and completed 806 transatlantic crossings.

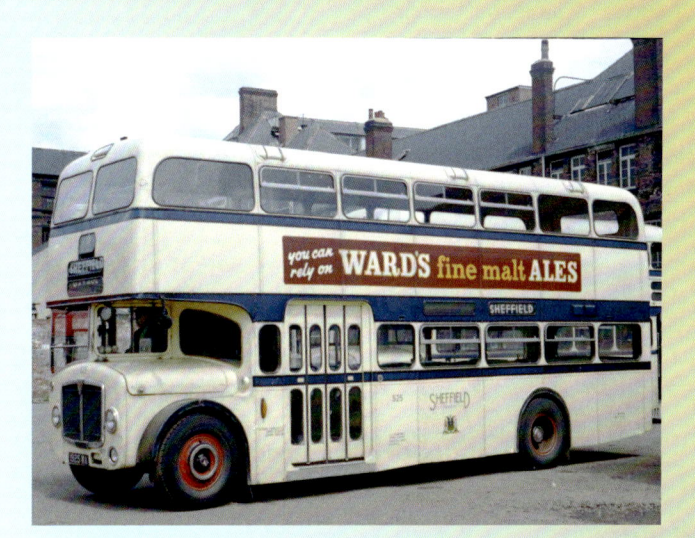

SHEFFIELD In April 1961 Sheffield took delivery of No 525 (1925 WA), a Park Royal-bodied AEC Bridgemaster, which entered service initially operating for a number of years on services 101 and 102 to Gleadless and Herdings; it later moved to the Dinnington services 6 and 19, where its low height enabled it to operate under the low railway bridge at South Aniston. This view was taken on 20 September 1969, with No 525 preparing to work service 19. Today the bus is in preservation with Yorkshire Heritage Trust. *Author's collection*

On this day the 18th Ryder Cup at Royal Birkdale ended in a 16-16 tie.

Photo	DESTINATIONS
28	HALFWAY
29	ATHERTON
30	LIVERPOOL
31	LIVERPOOL
32	LIVERPOOL
33	BIRKENHEAD
34	MANSFIELD
35	MANSFIELD
36	MANSFIELD
37	NOTTINGHAM
38	DERBY

HALFWAY Great Yarmouth bought six Albion NS3N Nimbus buses with Willowbrook B31F bodies in 1959, and between March and November 1965 five of them, CEX 490 to 494, were purchased second-hand by Booth & Fisher of Halfway, South Yorkshire. The company eventually assembled a collection of ten Nimbuses, two of which were new to the operator. This is CEX 490 at the Halfway House public house on 22 October 1969. *Author's collection*

On this day Led Zeppelin released **Led Zeppelin II,** *and three days later Pink Floyd released their album* **Ummagumma.**

Right: **ATHERTON** Despite buying six Daimler CRG6LXs in 1962, Lancashire United quickly returned to the tried and tested Guy Arab for its double-deck requirements. The operator continued to purchase Guy Arabs until 1968. In service to Atherton on 14 November 1969 is No 187 (RTC 352C), an NCME-bodied Guy Arab V new in 1965. *Author's collection*

Apollo 12, with astronauts Conrad, Gordon and Bean, was successfully launched on this day; five days later Conrad and Bean became the third and fourth humans to walk on the Moon. Apollo 12 returned home safely on 24 November.

Buses, Coaches & Recollections 1969

21

LIVERPOOL A total of 125 MCCW-bodied AEC Regent V D3RVs were delivered to Liverpool Corporation between 1956 and 1959. They all had AEC A218 9.6-litre engines and synchromesh gearboxes, and the engine bonnet, grille and built-up nearside wing, incorporating the sidelight, were to Liverpool's own specification. The bodywork was a four-bay version of Metro-Cammell's 'Orion' body, which had a seating capacity of 62, this being achieved by incorporating a rearward-facing bench seat for five at the front of the lower saloon. Thirty of these vehicles, Nos A203-A232, were delivered with MCCW body frames, the panelling and general finishing being completed by the Corporation's own workforce at Edge Lane Works. However, due to other commitments at the works, the last of the Liverpool-finished examples did not enter service until late 1959. This is No A219 (VKB 817) on 17 March 1969, one of the Liverpool Corporation-finished vehicles, which entered service in September 1959. *Author's collection*

On the day this view was taken the Longhope lifeboat was lost after answering a mayday call during severe storms in the Pentland Firth; all eight crew members perished.

LIVERPOOL

Between November 1962 and September 1964 200 Leyland PDR1s with Metro-Cammell bodywork were delivered to Liverpool Corporation. However, their large-scale introduction was delayed while the unions and the Corporation settled their differences over the use of bigger buses, so it was not until 4 February 1963 that the first routes, the 86 and 87 Pier Head to Garston Circular, were converted to Leyland PDR1 operation, and Nos L500 to L519 were allocated to Garston Garage for use on these routes. This is No L508 (508 KD), working route 87 on 30 January 1969. *Author's collection*

The Beatles gave their last public performance on the roof of Apple Records in London.

Right: **BIRKENHEAD** Standing at the Woodside bus/ferry terminal on 3 March 1969 is Birkenhead Corporation No 56 (LCM 456), an East Lancashire-bodied Leyland PD2/40 new in July 1961. *Author's collection*

On this day Jim Morrison of The Doors was arrested in Florida for indecent exposure during a Doors concert three days earlier.

Below left: **MANSFIELD** The last ECW-bodied Bristol LD6Gs delivered to Mansfield District arrived in 1959, and were numbered 520 to 524 (191 to 195 BRR). This is No 521 (192 BRR) on 17 August 1969. Apollo was Home Brewery's soft drinks brand. *Author's collection*

On this day the category 5 hurricane 'Camille', the most powerful tropical cyclonic system in history at landfall, hit the Mississippi coast, killing 248 people.

Below right: **MANSFIELD** En route to Bingham on 2 August 1969 is Mansfield District No 209 (SNN 71), an ECW-bodied Bristol LS6G new in 1955. It became the last of five LS6Gs from that year to remain in service with the operator, being sold to Gosport & Fareham in May 1970 for spares; it was broken up for scrap in September of that year. *Author's collection*

Buses, Coaches & Recollections 1969

Below: **NOTTINGHAM** All 28 buses of West Bridgford Urban District Council (all of AEC manufacture) passed to City of Nottingham Transport on 29 September 1968. In a short period of time 17 had been withdrawn, but among those retained were six East Lancashire-bodied AEC Regent Vs. Representing these on 7 June 1969 is Nottingham No 278 (335 GNN), which had been new in September 1960. All six were withdrawn in 1974 and, together with three others, No 278 was exported to British Columbia Hydro and Power Authority in Canada. *Author's collection*

On this day the rock group Blind Faith – Eric Clapton, Ginger Baker, Stevie Winwood and Ric Grech – played their first concert in London's Hyde Park in front of 100,000 people. The group disbanded in August 1969 after one album.

The No 1 single in late August 1969 was In The Year 2525 by Zager and Evans, and the No 1 album was Jethro Tull's Stand Up.

Above: **MANSFIELD** Heading for Nottingham on 23 September 1969 is Mansfield District/Midland General No 106 (FNN 163D), an ECW-bodied Bristol MW6G new in 1966. *Author's collection*

On this day Butch Cassidy and the Sundance Kid opened in the USA, starring Paul Newman, Robert Redford and one of my favourite actresses, Katherine Ross.

DERBY Leaving Derby bus station for the journey to Burton via Repton on 3 June 1969 is Blue Bus Services No DR17 (YRB 483), a low-height Willowbrook-bodied Daimler CVG6 new in 1955. On 21 December 1973 Blue Bus Services' vehicles were acquired by Derby Corporation, but just over three years later a disastrous fire at Willington Depot destroyed most of the smaller operator's vehicles, apart from one of the Dennis Lolines, 465 FRB, and YRB 483, which remained in the Derby fleet until early 1977, when it was sold for scrap. *Author's collection*

While operating at sea on SEATO manoeuvres on 3 June 1969, the Australian aircraft carrier HMAS Melbourne accidentally rammed and sliced in two the American destroyer USS Frank E. Evans in the South China Sea, killing 74 American seamen.

Buses, Coaches & Recollections 1969

Photo	DESTINATIONS
39	STAFFORD
40	LICHFIELD
41	WOLVERHAMPTON
42	WOLVERHAMPTON
43	BRIDGNORTH
44	WEST BROMWICH
45	COVENTRY
46	NORWICH
47	CAMBRIDGE
48	HITCHIN

STAFFORD Midland Red built two prototype D10 underfloor-engine double-deck buses, 963 KHA and 1944 HA. The latter, numbered 4944, entered service from Sheepcoat Street depot in Birmingham in April 1961 and was fitted with a narrow exit and a second staircase at the rear. The idea was to channel passenger flow by using the front door and staircase as an entrance only, with passengers leaving via the rear exit and staircase. This twin-stair, twin-door layout reduced the seating capacity to 65, and the positioning of the rear staircase required the rear emergency door be relocated to the traditional position in the centre. However, the experimental layout was not successful and in November 1962 the bus returned to Central Works and was rebuilt with a single front door and staircase. In April 1964 No 4944 was transferred to Stafford where it remained until its withdrawal in January 1973, and was unfortunately sold for scrap in June of that year. It is seen in Stafford on 14 September 1969. *Bob Gell*

On 26 September the Beatles released their album **Abbey Road.**

Right: **LICHFIELD** During June and July 1953 Walsall Corporation took delivery of ten Roe-bodied Leyland PD2/12s, Nos 811 to 820 (RDH 501 to 510). They were 27 feet long, had extra luggage space and were the first buses to be painted in the livery of light blue with yellow lining. This is No 812 (RDH 502) in Lichfield bus station on 21 July 1969. Between August 1959 and April 1960, together with Nos 811 and 813, this bus was lengthened to 28ft 11in with a slightly increased rear overhang, and converted by Willowbrook to a front entrance. No 812 passed to West Midlands Passenger Transport Executive (WMPTE) on 1 October 1969 and was sold for scrap in March 1972. *Bob Gell*

During a landmark TV broadcast on this day Neil Armstrong became the first man to walk on the Moon, saying 'That's one small step for a man, one giant leap for mankind' – or did he?

Left: **WOLVERHAMPTON** In October 1966 No 720 (KUK 720D) was bought new by Wolverhampton Corporation and was a most unusual bus for a municipal operator, being a Ford R226 with Strachans Pacesaver bodywork. It is seen here on 10 August 1969. *Bob Gell*

On 9 and 10 August the name Charles Manson would become known to millions, when actress Sharon Tate and four others were murdered in Beverly Hills.

Buses, Coaches & Recollections 1969

WOLVERHAMPTON This is Wolverhampton No 70 (4070 JW) on 10 August 1969, one of two Guy Wulfrunians owned and operated by the Corporation with bodywork by East Lancashire. No 70 first saw service on 1 January 1961, being extensively used on the Codsall services. It was delicensed on 28 June 1966 but reinstated on 1 January 1967, delicensed again on 26 June 1967, and again relicensed on 3rd February 1969. Taken into the ownership of the WMPTE on 1 October 1969, the bus was delicensed for the last time in December 1970. After standing on Oxford Street bus compound for many months, it was sold to Wombwell Diesels for scrap (minus its engine) in March 1972, and broken up. The least troublesome component of the bus was the engine, a Gardner 6LX. *Bob Gell*

BRIDGNORTH In mid-1967 Wolverhampton Corporation took delivery of six Strachan-bodied AEC Swifts, Nos 708 to 713 (NJW 708E to 713E). This view was taken on 10 August 1969 at Bridgnorth station, with the bus on a private hire. *Bob Gell*

On this day France devalued the franc by 12½%, producing a depression in the country, with President Charles de Gaulle openly criticised for his financial policies. Tourists, however, were very happy.

WEST BROMWICH One of my favourite Corporation liveries was West Bromwich, and carrying it on 11 June 1969 is No 248 (248 NEA), a Metro-Cammell-bodied Daimler CVG6-30 new in 1963. Daimler buses with Metro-Cammell bodies were a typical West Bromwich choice for many years, with CVG6s being purchased throughout the model's production period. The CVG6-30 version, 30 feet long, was introduced following relaxation of dimensions in 1956. Air brakes and the new 'Daimatic' electro-pneumatic gearbox were standard on the longer model and ideal for town work. West Bromwich bought 35 of these buses between 1958 and 1965; No 248 entered service on 11 October 1963 and passed to the WMPTE in 1969. It was transferred to Walsall in September 1973 and returned to Oak Lane, West Bromwich, in March 1976. In October it began a new career at Birmingham garages, moving to Hockley and, two months later, Liverpool Street. Its last months, from February to October 1978, were at Harborne. The BaMMOT Museum purchased No 248 at auction in December 1978. *Author's collection*

Buses, Coaches & Recollections 1969

COVENTRY In 1968 Coventry took delivery of 18 ECW-bodied Daimler CRG6LXs, Nos 23 to 40 (KWK 23F to 40F). These were the first Coventry buses to be equipped for one-person operation. Standing in Pool Meadow bus station on 30 June 1969 is No 25 (KWK 25F). During 1973 and 1974 all 18 were rebuilt to single-doorway operation, but retained the central staircase. *Bob Gell*

Six days before this view was taken the UK and Rhodesia severed diplomatic ties.

NORWICH Moving now to East Anglia, this is Eastern Counties No LKH 133 (HPW 133), an ECW-bodied Bristol K5G, photographed in Drayton Road, Norwich, on 1 April 1969. Loaned from new to London Transport in May 1949, this bus ran from 1950 to October 1969 operating from various depots, including Peterborough, King's Lynn and Norwich. It was sold through dealer Ben Jordan to Brookside Coaches, Market Deeping, in March 1970, then bought privately in 1973; it is currently kept at the Lincolnshire Vintage Vehicle Society's premises. *Author's collection*

The Hawker Siddeley Harrier jump jet entered service with the Royal Air Force on this day.

1969 Happenings (1)

January
Australian media magnate Rupert Murdoch buys *News of the World*
The 'Waverley' railway line, Edinburgh-Carlisle, closes to passengers
Soviet Union launches Soyuz 4 and 5, which link up in space for transfer of crew
Sir Matt Busby announces his retirement as manager of Manchester United after 24 years
Richard Nixon succeeds Lyndon Johnson as 37th President of the USA
Violent student protests close London School of Economics
Ford launches the Capri
Elvis Presley begins recording session that produces *Suspicious Minds* and *In the Ghetto*

February
Yasser Arafat elected leader of Palestine Liberation Organisation
Lulu marries Bee Gee Maurice Gibb
Mariner 6 Mars probe launched

March
First test flight of Concorde at Toulouse, France
NASA launches Apollo 9 to test lunar module
Kray twins found guilty of murder, Ronnie for killing George Cornell and Reggie for Jack 'the Hat' McVitie; both sentenced to life imprisonment
Paul McCartney marries Linda Eastman
Golda Meir becomes first female prime minister of Israel

Buses, Coaches & Recollections 1969

The No 1 singles in April were Marvin Gaye with I Heard It Through The Grapevine, Desmond Dekker with Israelites, and the Beatles with Get Back.

Below: **NEAR HITCHIN** En route to Hitchin at an unknown location on 24 April 1969 is United Counties No 119 (PNV 219), one of four ECW dual-purpose-bodied Bristol LS5Gs that were delivered in November 1957, but not licensed until June 1958. No 119 was reseated with bus seats in August 1969 and remained in the fleet until November 1974. It was later noted with the 1st Davenport Scouts, Stockport, in July 1975. *Author's collection*

British Leyland was created in 1968 and launched its first model, the Austin Maxi, in Portugal on 24 April 1969.

Above: **CAMBRIDGE** Burwell & District was a small company based in the Cambridgeshire village of that name, just north-west of Newmarket and 10 miles north-east of Cambridge. The company's first Fleetline, 9 DER, was a former demonstrator, and its Willowbrook body lacked the distinctive fluting on the front dash and the strengthening ribs on the roof. The second Willowbrook-bodied Daimler CRG6LX new to Burwell & District in November 1965, DEB 484C, was to full Coventry specification, including the style of the front destination and route indicators; this view was taken in Cambridge bus station on 10 April 1969. The car following the bus is a 1967-registered Hillman Imp. *Author's collection*

Buses, Coaches & Recollections 1969

Photo	DESTINATIONS
49	LONDON
50	LONDON
51	LONDON
52	LONDON
53	LONDON
54	LONDON
55	LONDON
56	HYTHE
57	BRIGHTON
58	SOUTHAMPTON
59	READING
60	SWINDON
61	CHELTENHAM
62	BRISTOL
63	TOTNES
64	DARTMOUTH
65	LOOE

LONDON On Ecclestone Bridge, Victoria, on 11 July 1969 is No RMC1455 (455 CLT), a Park Royal-bodied AEC Routemaster new in July 1962, when it entered service from Hertford depot working Greenline route 715A. In April 1967 it was overhauled at Aldenham and transferred to Windsor, where it was allocated when this view was taken, working route 718. In 1956 the 718 had been extended from Epping to Harlow New Town (Bus Station) via Thornwood and Potter Street. In 1962 the route had been converted to RMC-class short Routemaster coaches out of Harlow (HA) and Windsor (WR) garages, but was converted to one-person-operated single-deckers ten years later.

The overtaking bus is No RCL2233 (CUV 233C), a Park Royal-bodied AEC Routemaster that entered service from Romford depot in June 1965. In October 1968 it was transferred to Dunton Green to work routes 704 and 705, returning to Romford a few months after this view was taken, No 2233 passed to the London Transport Executive in December 1977. *Bob Gell*

Three days before this view was taken US troop withdrawal from Vietnam had begun.

Buses, Coaches & Recollections 1969

Left: **LONDON** In a crowded Victoria Coach Station, also on 11 July, is Grey Cars No 27 (EOD 27D), a Harrington-bodied AEC Reliance new in April 1966. The entire Grey Cars coach fleet would pass to Greenslades in May 1971, and No 27 would remain in that fleet until December 1975. *Bob Gell*

A day before this view was taken the trimaran of Donald Crowhurst, Teignmouth Electron, was found drifting and unoccupied. He had been attempting the Sunday Times Golden Globe race, a single-handed round-the-world yacht race.

Below right: **LONDON** Between 1962 and 1968 Eastern National purchased 15 Bristol FLF coaches for the X10 Southend to London express service and its variants, and for a number of years the coaches brought high standards of comfort and prestige to these express routes. By 1973, with the X10 demoted to a limited-stop service and one-man operation, the FLFs became surplus to requirements, but not yet life-expired. All except one were subsequently rebuilt as 70-seat buses and numbered 2932 to 2946. This is No 2604 (RWC 607), an ECW coach-bodied Bristol FLF6B new in 1963, in Victoria Coach Station working the X10 service on 28 March 1969. *Author's collection*

After a long illness the former United States General and President Dwight D. Eisenhower died on this day.

1969 Happenings (2)

March (continued)
Eurovision Song Contest in Madrid results in four co-winners – Spain, Netherlands, France and UK (Lulu singing *Boom Bang-a-bang*)

April
Representation of the People Act lowers voting age from 21 to 18 with effect from February 1970
British troops arrive in Northern Ireland to reinforce Royal Ulster Constabulary
Robin Knox-Johnston becomes first person to sail non-stop around the world
Final episode of long-running BBC radio serial *Mrs Dale's Diary*
Charles de Gaulle steps down as President of France after losing referendum

May
NASA launches Apollo 10 as eight-day 'full dress rehearsal' for manned Moon landing

June
BBC documentary *The Royal Family* attracts almost 31 million viewers, an all-time British record for a non-current events programme
Patrick Troughton bows out as second Doctor Who; his final episode is last to be recorded in black and white

July
Prince Charles is invested as Prince of Wales at Caernarfon

LONDON Entering service in April 1966, Nos XMS1 to XMS6 (JLA 51D to 56D) were Strachan-bodied AEC Merlins that operated the new Red Arrow 500 service. This is No XMS6 (JLA 56D) at Victoria railway station on 11 July 1969. A couple of months later the bus was stored in Bexleyheath before going to Aldenham, where it was reseated, reclassified MB6 and repainted. It then passed to Muswell Hill for storage, after which it was transferred to Enfield to work on route 107. Three months later it was in store again at Poplar, and after very sporadic use at Wood Green it returned to storage at Poplar, prior to withdrawal in August 1973. The bus was later sold to Violet Bus Services in Dundalk, and was destroyed in January 1978. *Bob Gell*

On this day David Bowie released Space Oddity.

Below left: **LONDON** Working service 11 in Buckingham Palace Road, Victoria, on 1 September 1969 is No RM1737 (737 DYE), a Park Royal-bodied AEC Routemaster that entered service at Cricklewood depot in November 1963; it was quickly transferred to New Cross depot and remained there until August 1969. In that month at Aldenham the bus received an all-over advert for Silexine Paints and became the first all-over advert bus in London, based at Hammersmith depot. *Bob Gell*

On this day a coup in Libya ousted King Idris and brought Colonel Gaddafi to power.

Opposite top left: **LONDON** In Trafalgar Square on 5 October 1969 is No RTW73 (KGK 573), an all-Leyland PD2/3 that entered service from Shepherds Bush depot in September 1949. After a number of depot changes, the bus was stored at Riverside depot in February 1964; the following month it was converted to a driver trainer, and was employed as such until December 1969, when it was stored again before being sold for scrap eight months later. *Bob Gell*

On this day Monty Python's Flying Circus first aired on BBC1.

Buses, Coaches & Recollections 1969

here is No XA38 (JLA 38D), which entered service from Highgate depot in January 1966 on service 271. Three months later it was transferred to East Grinstead for services 424, 435 and 438C. In July 1966 No XA38 was transferred to Stamford Hill for service 67, then to Tottenham for service 76. Working that service on 2 October 1969, the bus is seen alongside the Bank of England; shortly afterwards it was overhauled at Aldenham, which included conversion to one-person operation. Transferred to Croydon in April 1970, No XA38 remained there until January 1973, when it was sold to the China Bus Company, together with the 49 other Atlanteans. *Bob Gell*

Below right: **HYTHE** In March 1967 East Kent took delivery of ten Marshall-bodied Bedford VAS1s (KJG 104E to 113E). Representing this batch is KJG 105E at Hythe on 20 March 1969. In July 1972 this bus was converted to an executive vehicle with 18 reclining seats and fitted carpets. By February 1977 it had passed to Staines of Brentwood. The bus behind it is KFN 240, a Weymann dual-purpose-bodied AEC Reliance new in 1955, which remained in the fleet until April 1976, when it was sold for scrap. *Author's collection*

In Gibraltar on this day, John Lennon and Yoko Ono were married and proceeded to their honeymoon bed-in for peace in Amsterdam.

Right: **LONDON** London Transport purchased 50 Leyland PDR1/1s for extensive trials, with bodywork based on a design by Park Royal developed for Stockton Corporation. They had a transverse Leyland O.680 11.1-litre engine driving through a fluid flywheel with an automatic gearbox. The first was delivered to Aldenham in July 1965 and the trials began in November. Seen

BRIGHTON Delivered in June 1963 and entering service with Brighton Corporation on 1 July were Nos 25 to 27 (25 to 27 CCD), Metro-Cammell Weymann-bodied Leyland PD2/37s. No 25 was converted to one-person operation in July 1966 and re-entered service in September. It is seen here on 9 April 1969. The rather tired-looking car in the foreground is a Ford Consul Classic, which was available new between 1961 and 1964, when it was replaced by the Corsair. *Author's collection*

Concorde 002 was the second prototype and was assembled in Britain. It made its maiden flight from the British Aircraft Corporation's plant at Filton, Bristol, on this day.

SOUTHAMPTON Not the most shapely of buses, this is Southampton No 302 (302 TR), a Park Royal-bodied Leyland PD2/27 and one of a batch of 12 new in March 1961. Photographed on 31 July 1969, it was out of service by late 1972 and was sold to Limebourne Limited of London, which converted it to open-top form in July 1977. The car heading towards the camera is a 1969 Rolls Royce Silver Shadow, which, when first produced in 1965, cost £6,557. *Author's collection*

From 1 August 1969 the halfpenny coin ceased to be legal tender in the UK.

READING A batch of ten Burlingham-bodied AEC Reliances was delivered to Reading in January 1959 (Nos 11 to 14, PRD 31 to 34) and October 1959 (Nos 15 to 20, SRD 15 to 20). They were renumbered 211 to 220 in December 1968, and carrying its new number on 6 July 1969 is No 216 (SRD 16). It passed to Reading Borough Transport in April 1974 and remained in that fleet until July 1978, when it was sold via a dealer to Phillips Coach Company, Shiptonthorpe. *Author's collection*

Francisco Franco ordered the closing of the border and communications between Gibraltar and Spain.

Below: **SWINDON** During March 1956 Swindon Corporation took delivery of 12 Park Royal-bodied Daimler CVG6s, Nos 85 to 96 (MMR 885 to 896). Representing this batch on 15 July 1969 is a freshly repainted No 87 (MMR 887), standing in Fleming Way with the bus station in the background. No 87 would be transferred to Thamesdown Transport on 1 April 1974 and remained in that fleet until August 1975. *Author's collection*

Buses, Coaches & Recollections 1969

Above: **CHELTENHAM** In 1969 Black & White took delivery of ten Plaxton Panorama Elite Daimler Roadliner SRP8s, Nos D300 to D309 (RDG 300G to 309G). They were fitted with Perkins V8 engines and lasted in the fleet until 1975, when many found new homes all around the UK. This is No 304 (RDG 304G) in Cheltenham coach station on 30 June 1969. *Bob Gell*

The following day Charles Philip Arthur George was invested as the Prince of Wales at Caernarfon Castle.

Right: **BRISTOL** Bristol's No 2910 (XHW 426), an ECW-bodied Bristol LS5G, entered service in June 1957 and was at first a regular performer on the Bath City routes 17/18 for about five years. In January 1959 it was converted to one-person operation and remained allocated to Bath depot until February 1973. Working a Trowbridge service, this view was taken on 20 June 1969; No 2910 is now safe in preservation in Stroud, not too far from its former home. Standing alongside is No 2934, an ECW-bodied Bristol MW5G new in October 1958. *Author's collection*

On this day Georges Pompidou was elected President of France.

Below right: **TOTNES** The Bristol SU was the successor to the SC chassis and, of the more than 180 produced, Southern and Western National took no fewer than 133 examples. It had an Albion EN250 four-cylinder engine, a David Brown gearbox, a Kirkstall front axle, a BMC rear axle and servo-assisted brakes. The SU was to be found in every corner of Western National's territory, and gave sterling service, being especially well suited to the narrow rural roads of the West Country. Leaving Totnes for Paignton on 11 June 1969 is ECW-bodied Bristol SUL4A No 637 (351 EDV). It was withdrawn and sold to Swanbrook of Staverton in February 1972 and was still noted with that operator in November 1978. *Bob Gell*

The No 1 album at the time of this view was Bob Dylan's Nashville Skyline.

Right: **DARTMOUTH** At the terminus of the Dartmouth-Townstal service 90 in Dartmouth on 11 June 1969 is Western National No 1872 (OTT 11), an ECW-bodied Bristol LD6B new in 1954. It would become a tree-lopper in December 1971. *Bob Gell*

Eight days before this view was taken the last episode of the original Star Trek TV series, 'Turnabout Intruder', was aired on NBC.

Below: **LOOE** Court Coaches of Torquay purchased three new Duple Bella Vega-bodied Bedford SB5s in April and May 1967 (JTA 763E to 765E). The company was acquired by Devon General in October 1970 and for a time the coaches ran in the Court livery seen in this view of JTA 765E in Looe on 13 June 1969. All three vehicles passed to Greenslades in May 1971, remaining there until late 1974/early 1975. This bus passed to Turner of Chulmleigh in January 1975, where it stayed for a further ten years. The Bedford on the right, 950 HPT, is a Duple-bodied SB1 that went new to Iveson of Cornsay Colliery, Durham. *Bob Gell*

A few days after this photograph was taken Judy Garland died of a drugs overdose in her London home.

Buses, Coaches & Recollections 1969

Wales

Photo	DESTINATIONS
66	ABERGAVENNY
67	ABERAVON
68	ABERAVON
69	CARDIFF
70	BRITON FERRY
71	TEDEGAR
72	GELLIGAER
73	GELLIGAER
74	GELLIGAER
75	BEDWAS
76	GUERNESEY

ABERGAVENNY We now move to Wales, and on 29 June 1969 this Yeates-bodied AEC Reliance (26 MTF) was photographed in Abergavenny. Purchased by Shipley of Ashton-under-Lyne in 1960, it is seen here in the ownership of Chiltern Queens of Woodcote. *Bob Gell*

Films released in June 1969 were Death Rides a Horse, Carry on Camping, The Wild Bunch *and* True Grit. *One of my favourite songs of this year was at No 4 in the charts,* Time is Tight *by Booker T and the MGs.*

ABERAVON In August 1940 Brighton, Hove & District took delivery of No 6351 (CAP 205), an ECW-bodied Bristol K5G. It was rebuilt with an open top in the early 1950s and was purchased by Thomas Bros (Port Talbot) Ltd in 1960; it is seen at that company's depot on 28 June 1969. On the right is GHT 127, a similar K5G new in March 1941 as Bristol's No C3315, a replacement for the last of the Bristol trams; it was withdrawn in 1954 and sold to Brighton, Hove & District as an open-top bus in November 1955. It was purchased by Thomas Bros in May 1965 and remained with the company until December 1969, when it returned to the Bristol Omnibus Company. *Bob Gell*

On this day John Hampshire scored 107 on his Test cricket debut at Lord's against the West Indies.

ABERAVON Port Talbot and Aberavon never had a municipal operator, and local services were provided by Thomas Bros. To maintain these services a batch of 18 Leyland PSUC1/1 Tiger Cubs was purchased new by the company in 1954; registered NNY 54 to 71, nine were bodied by Weymann and nine by Saunders-Roe. Representing the latter batch is NNY 70, and on the right is TTG 4, a Weymann-bodied Tiger Cub new in 1956. By the time this view was taken, on 28 June 1969, control of Thomas Bros had passed to South Wales Transport, in April. *Bob Gell*

CARDIFF Rhondda purchased six Northern Counties-bodied Leyland PDR1/1s in September 1968, numbered 496 to 501. This is No 501 (RTX 501G) at Cardiff bus station on 28 June 1969; note the damage to the front panel on a bus that is only ten months old. *Bob Gell*

Top right: **BRITON FERRY** From 1930 to 1971 Neath & Cardiff Luxury Coaches ran an express service from Swansea via Neath to Cardiff. Control of the company passed to South Wales Transport in April 1969, but the company was not fully absorbed until 1 January 1971. In November 1966 Neath & Cardiff purchased from Trent two Weymann-bodied AEC Reliance coaches, RRC 237 and 238, and allocated them the fleet numbers 106 and 107. Standing at N&C's Briton Ferry depot on 28 June 1969 is No 106; by October 1971 it had been sold for scrap, minus its engine. In 1969 Cardiff was the only capital city in Great Britain that banned X-rated films on a Sunday. *Bob Gell*

A few days after this view was taken, on 3 July 1969, Swansea was granted city status.

Below: **TREDEGAR** Also photographed on 29 June 1969 was UNY 831G, a Plaxton bodied AEC Reliance new to Neath & Cardiff in March of that year. Later this bus was one of six AEC Reliances acquired by Western Welsh on 1 January 1971 as part of its share of the Neath & Cardiff express route from Cardiff to Swansea; it would be sold to Ensign of Grays in November 1978, then passed to J. M. Lewington, Harold Hill, in June 1980. *Bob Gell*

Buses, Coaches & Recollections 1969

The Stonewall Riot in New York City on 28 June 1969 marked the beginning of the gay rights movement.

GELLIGAER In the red, white and green livery introduced by Roy Marshall, the General Manager of Gelligaer UDC, this is No 36 (STB 957C), a Willowbrook-bodied Leyland PSUR1/1R new in 1965 as a demonstrator, and purchased from Leyland Motors in 1967. This picture was also taken on 29 June 1969. No 36 was withdrawn in 1972 and was purchased through a dealer by Conway Hunt of Ottershaw in September of that year. Later, in the livery of Conway Hunt, it was noted with Keenan of Coalhall in July 1977. *Bob Gell*

GELLIGAER lies north of Caerphilly, and this is the Urban District Council's No 35 (FGW 498C), a Willowbrook-bodied AEC Swift that was built as a demonstrator for AEC in 1965, and acquired by Gelligaer in 1967. This view, taken on 29 June 1969, shows No 35 painted white with green wheels for the Investiture of the Prince of Wales, which took place at Caernarfon Castle on 1 July. *Bob Gell*

A couple of days after this view was taken the Dinorwic slate quarry in Snowdonia closed. It was the second largest slate quarry in the world, and at its peak covered more than 700 acres. The site is now home to the National Slate Museum.

GELLIGAER Also seen on the same occasion, in the old Gelligaer livery of red, green and grey, is No 34 (LTG 734D), one of two Willowbrook-bodied AEC Reliances new in 1966. They were the first to be delivered new with electric doors; in December 1971 both were converted to single-door entrance/exit. *Bob Gell*

1969 Happenings (3)

July (continued)

- First US troop withdrawals from Vietnam take place
- NASA launches Apollo 11 (Neil Armstrong, Buzz Aldrin and Michael Collins) to achieve the first Moon landing on the 21st, watched by an estimated TV audience of 500 million; they return safely on the 24th
- Edward Kennedy drives off a bridge at Chappaquiddick Island, Massachusetts; his passenger, Mary Jo Kopechne, dies
- Spanish dictator Francisco Franco appoints Prince Juan Carlos as his successor

Buses, Coaches & Recollections 1969

BEDWAS and Machen are small townships on the main road between Caerphilly and Newport, and the Council began operating a bus service to Caerphilly in 1922. Until 1947 no double-deck buses were owned, but by 1969 the fleet consisted of five double-deckers and a single-decker, and at this time was the second smallest municipal fleet in the UK. This is No 5 (422 CAX), a Massey-bodied AEC Regent V new in 1961 and photographed on a wet 12 August 1969. *Author's collection*

On this day BBC2 aired the first Pot Black snooker tournament.

Guernsey

GUERNSEY Motors and Guernsey Railways were a jointly run company that for a number of years used different liveries for the two branches of the company, red with cream trim for Motors and green with cream trim for Railways. Photographed on 15 August 1969 this is No 51 (6441), a railway-operated Heaver-bodied Albion Victor new in 1953. John Thomas Heaver set up in business by 1920 and was always a small coachbuilder; in the 1930s Bedfords with small coach and bus bodies were supplied to a number of operators. The company moved into full-front bodywork on front-engine chassis in the early 1950s, building a large number of bodies for Guernsey, mainly on the Albion Victor chassis. *Author's collection*

The Woodstock Festival began on this day and ran for three days.

1969 Happenings (4)

August
- Mariner 7 passes within 3,500km of Mars
- Violence erupts following march by Apprentice Boys of Derry, resulting in three days of rioting dubbed the 'Battle of Bogside'; British troops deployed to Northern Ireland
- Second Isle of Wight Festival attracts 150,000 people, an appearance by Bob Dylan being a major draw

September
- First 'automated teller machine' ('hole-in-the-wall' cash machine) in USA installed in New York
- Iconic 1960s fashion store Biba reopens on Kensington High Street, London
- Very last theatrical Warner Bros cartoon is released – 'Merrie Melodies' short 'Injun Trouble'

October
- New seven-sided 50p coin, introduced as replacement for 10-shilling note, has mixed reception from public

1969 Arrivals & Departures

Arrivals

Michael Schumacher	Racing driver	3 January
Marilyn Manson	Rock musician	5 January
Stephen Hendry	Snooker player	13 January
Jennifer Aniston	American actress	11 February
Javier Bardem	Spanish actor	1 March
Alexander McQueen	Fashion designer	17 March
Cerys Matthews	Singer	11 April
Dion Dublin	Footballer	22 April
Renée Zellweger	Actress	22 April
Tess Daly	TV presenter	27 April
Wes Anderson	Film director	1 May
Brian Lara	West Indian cricketer	2 May
Eagle Eye Cherry	Swedish-born musician	7 May
Dennis Bergkamp	Dutch footballer	10 May
Cate Blanchett	Actress	14 May
Steffi Graf	Tennis player	14 June
Ice Cube	Rapper/actor	14 June
Jennifer Lopez	Actress/singer	24 July
Edward Norton	Actor	18 August
Christian Slater	Actor	18 August
Matthew Perry	Actor	19 August
Jack Black	Actor/musician	28 August
Shane Warne	Australian cricketer	13 September
Catherine Zeta Jones	Actress	25 September
Gwen Stefani	Singer	3 October
Steve McQueen	Film director	9 October
Ernie Els	South African golfer	17 October
Matthew McConaughey	Actor	4 November
Gerard Butler	Actor	13 November
Richard Hammond	TV presenter	19 December
Ed Miliband	Politician	24 December

Departures

Richmal Crompton	Author, creator of 'William' (b.1890)	11 January
Irene Castle	Dancer (b1893)	25 January
Boris Karloff	Actor (b1887)	2 February
Thelma Ritter	Actress (b1902)	4 February
Conrad Hilton Jnr	US heir and socialite(b1926)	5 February
Kenneth Horne	Comedian (b1907)	14 February
John Wyndham	Author (b1903)	11 March
Billy Cotton	British entertainer & bandleader (b1899)	25 March
Dwight D. Eisenhower	US President (b1890)	28 March
Osbert Sitwell	Writer (b1892)	4 May
Robert Taylor	Actor (b1911)	8 June
Martita Hunt	Actress (b1899)	13 June
Judy Garland	Actress/singer (b1922)	22 June
Brian Jones	Rock musician (b1942)	3 July
Walter Gropius	German Architect (b1883)	5 July
Frank Loesser	US songwriter (b1910)	26 July
Dame Ivy Compton-Burnett	Novelist (b1884)	27 August
Rocky Marciano	Boxer (b1923)	31 August
Ho Chi Minh	President of Vietnam (b1890)	2 September
Gavin Maxwell	Naturalist/author (b1914)	7 September
Sonja Henie	Figure-skater (b1912)	12 October
Jack Kerouac	US author (b1922)	21 October
Ted Heath	Bandleader (b1902)	18 November
Eric Portman	Actor (b1901)	7 December

1969 Happenings (5)

October (continued)
- First message sent over 'ARPANET', forerunner of Internet

November
- *Sesame Street* is broadcast for first time, on USA's National Educational Television network
- NASA launches Apollo 12, successful second manned mission to the Moon
- 'Wendy' burger chain established in Columbus, Ohio, named after the nickname of founder Dave Thomas's daughter Melinda Lou
- First broadcast of BBC children's animation series *Clangers*, created by Oliver Postgate and Peter Firmin's Smallfilms
- *Sun* newspaper is relaunched as tabloid under ownership of Rupert Murdoch
- Soccer great Pelé scores his 1,000th goal

December
- Free concert is hosted by Rolling Stones at Altamont Speedway, California; ensuing violence viewed by many as 'the end of the Sixties'
- Death penalty for murder abolished by the UK Parliament
- Sixth James Bond film, *On Her Majesty's Secret Service*, released, starring George Lazenby and Diana Rigg

Index of Operators and Vehicles

Bedwas & Machen UDC: 422 CAX 45
Birkenhead: LCM 456 24
Black & White: RDG 304G 39
Blue Bus Services: YRB 483 26
Booth & Fisher (Halfway): CEX 490 20
Brighton: 25 CCD 38
Bristol: XHW 426, 924 AHY 39
Burwell & District: DEB 484C 33

Chiltern Queens (Woodcote): 26 MTF 41
Connor & Graham: OCD 776 13
County Motors: 3283 HE 18
Court Coaches (Torquay): JTA 765E
Coventry: KWK 25F 31

Dumfries: TCS 160 1
Dundee: CTS 629 4; CTS 631, CTS 127D 5

East Kent: KJG 105E, KFN 240 37
East Yorkshire: SRH 632 11; SRH 631, 9726 AT 12
Eastern Counties: HPW 133 32
Eastern National: RWC 607 35

Gelligaer UDC: FGW 498C, STB 957C 43; LTG 734D 44
Green Line: 455 CLT, CUV 233C 34
Grey Cars: EOD 27D 35
Guernsey Railways: 6441 46

Hull: BDJ 66, FRH 408D 9; OKH 341 10; OTV 142 11

Lancashire United: RTC 352C 21
Leeds: 576 CNW 14
Leith (Sanquhar): DRN 280 8
Liverpool: VKB 817 22; 508 KD 23
London: JLA 56D, 737 DYE 36; KGK 573, JLA 38D 37

McGill's (Barrhead): CHS 723C 6
Mansfield District/Midland General: FNN 163D 25
Mansfield District: 192 BRR, SNN 71 24
Midland Red: 1944 HA 27

Neath & Cardiff: RRC 237, UNY 831G 42

Reading: SRD 16 38
Rhondda: RTX 501G 42

Sheffield JOC: TWE 114F, 6308 W, 1925 WA 19
Southampton: 302 TR 38
Swindon: MMR 887 38

Thomas Bros (Port Talbot): CAP 205, GHT 127 41; NNY 70, TTG 4 42
Todmorden: HWY 36 18

United Counties: PNV 219 33

Walsall: RDH 502 28
West Bridgford UDC: 335 GNN 25
West Bromwich: 248 NEA 30
West Riding: BHL 380C 13; THL 895, RWY 516F 16
West Yorkshire: OWT 201 17
Western National: OTT 11 40
Western SMT: GCS 234 6; LCS 972 6; RAG 408, VCS 427 7
Wolverhampton: KUK 720D 28; 4070 JW, NJW 713E 29

Yorkshire Traction: RHE 448G 15; NCX 178 18
Yorkshire Woollen: KHD 408 15; UTF 930 17

Front cover: **LONDON** The church in the background is St John's, Waterloo, designed by Francis Octavius Bedford and built between 1822 and 1824. Working route 4A to Finsbury Park Station on 11 July 1969 is No RT3097 (KXW 206), an AEC Regent III that entered service in March 1950 from Catford depot with a Weymann body. In August 1965 the bus was overhauled at Aldenham and received a Park Royal body. At the time this view was taken, it was working out of Holloway depot; it was withdrawn from service in January 1973 and sold for scrap. *Bob Gell*